MW01065773

HARD BARGAIN

To the Zithis—
Thank you for sharing
your gifted son

Ken

HARD BARGAIN

Life-lessons from prostate cancer . . . a love story

KENNETH BRIGHAM, M.D.

HARPETH HOUSE
Nashville, Tennessee

This is a Harpeth House Book
Published by Harpeth House Publishing

Copyright by Kenneth Brigham, M.D.
All rights reserved under International and Pan-American
Copyright conventions. Published in the United States by Harpeth House Publishing,
Nashville

Library of Congress Cataloguing-in-Publication Data

Brigham,Kenneth
Hard Bargain: Life-lessons From Prostate Cancer, A Love Story/Kenneth Brigham, M.D.
p   cm.
ISBN: 0-9705692-0-3
1. Cancer
2. Prostate Cancer
1. Title
2001

Manufactured in the United States of America

First Edition

This book is dedicated to

Dr. Arlene Audray Stecenko

who saved my life

FOREWORD

This book was not meant for public consumption.
I have seen enough people resort to denial when
faced with their mortality to know that denial doesn't
work. Words written down, real words about real
times, places, people, and events, are difficult to deny;
there is something enduringly credible about words
written down. So, when told I had cancer, I resolved to
write down everything I could about the experience,
trying to make the words fit the feelings. It will be
obvious to anyone who reads what is here that it is the
unexpurgated version. I wrote what I was feeling as
clearly as I could, and this is it.

If you are a man and you live long enough, you
will have prostate cancer. If you are a woman and you
live long enough, someone you love will have prostate
cancer. That will continue to be true until someone
can figure out why it happens and how to prevent it.

Someone will figure those things out, but probably not soon enough to benefit most people who will read this.

As cancers go, this is a strange one. Prostate cancer cells are out of control, like all cancerous cells, but just barely; they grow slowly. But they grow inexorably, and this cancer will kill you if you don't die of something else first.

Because prostate cancer is insidious, it is easy to deny. Men don't want to know that their PSA is increasing and don't have to know for a long time. So, even with such a simple and sensitive blood test for early detection (maybe because of the sensitivity of the test), most of these cancers are discovered too late for a sure cure. Most men, even knowing they are at risk, just don't get the test, don't want to know.

I hope this book will change your mind about that. It is possible to delay dealing with reality, but reality in this case is not static—the reality gets a lot worse with time. And the reality can be dealt with, the tragedy experienced, without losing your sense of humor. Also, crises of this sort can nurture relationships. If there is a single most important lesson here it is that relationships are what you really care about, whether you admit it or not.

When I told my daughter, Heather, that publishing this book would be like undressing in public, she said, "No, it's a lot worse." She is right. There is a great deal of privacy invaded here, mine and some others. So why do it?

I thought that men who have this terribly common disease, and those who care for them, might benefit from another's experience. I am a physician and feel both the obligation and the desire to help people deal with disease. I thought that there might be comfort in the realizing that mortality is a universal phenomenon and that there are some positive effects of admitting that. I also learned a lot about myself and about priorities from the experience, and I thought those things might be worth telling to a broader audience.

However, I doubt that my motives were entirely pure. When I and others read what I wrote, we thought it was good writing. I like that. I hope the broader audience agrees.

KLB
SEPTEMBER 4, 2000
Nashville

FRIDAY
MAY 10, 1996
Nashville

I have cancer.

I just talked with Jay Smith on the phone, and he told me that. Finally, after a year and a half of sodomizing me repeatedly with his ultrasonic dildo and chipping away at my prostate gland, he hit pay dirt.

Arlene and I are leaving for New Orleans in fifteen or twenty minutes to attend the American Thoracic Society International Conference. I am a big deal there. I was the president. When I was the president, I did not have cancer.

This is harder than I thought it would be. It is not a surprise. My father died of prostate cancer when I was fifteen. The disease is no stranger. My PSA* has been on the rise for over a year. The damn thing was there. I knew it. Jay knew it. One time I said to him, "Why don't you just take it out?"

*prostate specific antigen, a blood test for early detection of prostate cancer

11

"You operate on a cancer, not a PSA," Jay said. "We have to find it first."

So this is not a big surprise. But that doesn't matter, doesn't soften the blow of finality, irrevocability. I have cancer. I am not the same person I was fifteen minutes ago, before I had cancer.

I feel what I felt when my mother died. She was sick and demented for some years, and her death was expected and was a blessing. I sat all night with her the last night of her life and held her hand and told her everything I could think of that I wished I had told her when she could hear it. I was ready, I thought, for her to die.

But the finality, the irrevocability. "Your mother is dead." "You have cancer." I sobbed. My heart hollowed out and left a frightening space in my chest.

Arlene held me for a while, and we flew to New Orleans.

SATURDAY
MAY 11
New Orleans

Arlene always finds these interesting, small, elegant bed-and-breakfasts when we travel. She doesn't do big chain things–not hotels, not restaurants–no chains, nothing that revolves.

The one she chose for us in New Orleans is just off Esplanade, a little too far out, past the freeway, a good mile and a half from the French Quarter. The proprietor is Victor. The place is a redone old residence—redone a la Victor. It is beautifully renovated, then decorated with a most god-awful collection of tasteless (probably not inexpensive, but tasteless even for New Orleans) art, furniture (a Barcalounger couch in the Picasso suite), and objets d'art. The Picasso suite has a pencil drawing of a face allegedly signed by Picasso. It looks like nothing Picasso ever did. Arlene and I joke that it must have been drawn by a local plumber named Herman Picasso.

We love traveling together, doing everything together, really. So much joy in the past five years. I would not have believed it possible. Beautifully exquisite cancerless joy. Does the cancer really matter? Right now it matters more than anything else in the world.

Victor is an oversolicitous boor. But he has an open bar. I avail myself of Victor's open bar.

Bella Luna last night, a late dinner. Arlene, myself, and my cancer. I guess Bella Luna must mean beautiful moon or something like that (maybe "deliriously crazy"; I like that better). Some years ago, before I was happy, I thought it would be wonderful to be crazy, to have a socially acceptable excuse for behaving badly in public. I wanted to be crazy but found myself incurably sane. That curse weighs heavily at the moment.

We sat at a banquette in a corner overlooking the river and ate beautifully. We held hands a lot. We laughed less and with more effort than usual. One of cancer's several evils is that it swallows laughter.

Today is Mother's Day. My daughter, Heather, always calls Arlene on Mother's Day to wish her happiness. Heather is twenty-two. She does not think of Arlene as her mother, but Heather is a caring woman and, I think, values Arlene as an adult, sane friend; God knows Heather has not been blessed with many of those. When I check messages at home, Heather has called twice and asked me to call her in New York. I would have thought she was just calling to wish Arlene happy Mother's Day but for the urgency and an edge to her voice that I know intimately as a plea for help. I call her Manhattan apartment; no answer. I leave a message. I will have to introduce Heather to my new friend, but it will be very difficult.

When I was much younger and lived in Scottsdale, escaping the Vietnam War by doing time in an outpost of the Communicable Disease Center (the Yellow Berets), I had a friend who said that he thought the garbage disposal a most elegant metaphor for God: the ultimate omnivore. Maybe not. Maybe cancer is God, cells slipping the bonds of mortality and soaring off without regard for any of the constraints that keep decent cells behaving well, each malignant cell a little piece of God. *Heather, I'm afraid we've found a little piece of God in my prostate gland that I must deal with. Not to worry.* Bullshit!

Arlene and I get out early for us and go see Kent Shih's poster presentation. Kent is a medical student who did an outstanding research project in Arlene's lab with some of my help. He does a superior job with the poster. We are proud.

Then we wander down to the Quarter and have Mother's Day brunch at Broussard's on Conti. We talk a lot about my cancer. We know too much and too little. We are both physicians, faculty at Vanderbilt. We mostly do research, but we are clinicians, too: pulmonologists. Arlene is a pediatrician, so prostates have not been a major issue for her. I watched my father die of prostate cancer when I was fifteen and learned more than I ever wanted to know about the disease from that experience. In my subsequent medical training, I think I avoided the gland as much as possible.

But we know some. We know there is an operation called a radical prostatectomy that leaves one usually cured, often impotent, and sometimes incontinent. I am fifty-six. Arlene is forty-five. Except for this, we are both in perfect health. We run fifteen or twenty miles a week. We like sex. I do not relish the thought of dribbling urine down my pants leg. I do not want to die. Arlene does not want me to die. I don't like any of the options I know about.

There is a white piano behind me where a too-blonde woman sits playing *Mona Lisa*. The wine steward spills champagne from Arlene's glass. The waiter talks too loud and too often. Arlene looks especially beautiful this afternoon.

We are supposed to stay at the meetings in New Orleans until Wednesday, but we decide to return to Nashville early. I want to go home. I want some time alone with Arlene and also to get the gory details directly from Jay Smith. We will go home tomorrow morning.

Heather called the hotel several times while we were out. I call her. She tells me tearfully that she and Daniel are separating. I am surprised.

Heather is married to Daniel Baldwin. Daniel is David Baldwin's son. David is James Baldwin's brother, a fact of understandably major significance in the lives of all Baldwins. Daniel was raised by his Jewish mother on the upper East side of New York. He spent time in Provence with his father, "uncle Jimmy," and assorted glitterati, but he was raised by his very white Jewish mother.

Daniel is not white; that is, he does not look white. He is a beautiful soft brown color with a mass of carefully coifed dreadlocks. He is a gifted artist, as best I can tell. I like Daniel.

Heather met Daniel at Oberlin College, during the time when her mother and I were going through a rancorous divorce. Heather and Daniel fell in love, Heather dropped out of school and moved with Daniel to New York. A year or so later they were married. I did not want them to marry because I thought them both too young and immature. At the time I was not especially enamored of the concept of marriage as an institution. But I accepted it, and I have done everything I know to do to support them.

I love Heather very much, and my heart breaks when I feel her pain. She is in pain. My heart is breaking. Arlene holds me close, and we do not speak.

Somewhere, deep in my pelvis, a little piece of God smiles wryly.

MONDAY
MAY 13
Nashville

It is one o'clock in the afternoon, and we are home. Home is a renovated floor in a former warehouse in Printer's Alley, an old night life district in the middle of the city. Our neighbors are Skull Schulman (owner of Skull's Rainbow Room, a venerable Alley bar), Lonnie, Malcolm (also Alley bar proprietors), and others who come and go without making much of an impression. And Jack and Barbara Norman. Jack is a prominent attorney and lives in an elegant flat above his office where both he and his wife Barbara work. Before he went to law school, Jack ran a circus and was married once to a trapeze artist. I love our home. It is the only home I have known as an adult. Heather has said more than once that she has no home, no roots. It bothers her. I understand at last. Arlene gave me a home.

We decide we want to talk with Jay Smith as soon as possible, and he can see us today at four o'clock. I am scared. I touch Arlene a lot and tell her I'm afraid. She understands. She is frightened, too.

Jay Smith is very good at what he does. He is

candid, but sympathetic. He treats me as he would any patient, not like another doctor. I am reassured. Doctors often get terrible medical care because they get "special" treatment from their peers. Jay gives everybody the same special treatment.

I have cancer. It is an intermediate grade based on the microscopic examination of the tissue and my PSA (now up in the 20s; normal is less than 3). There are four options:

1) <u>Do nothing</u>. Prostate cancers grow very slowly. I would likely live five years or more even if I did nothing. I am fifty-six years old now and otherwise in perfect health. I do not want to live five years. I want to live a lot longer than that. Arlene agrees. We will do something.

2) <u>External irradiation</u>. This works. The cure rate is somewhat less than surgery, but it is non-invasive. The incidence of impotence is eventually about the same as with surgery. The radiation treatments virtually always cause inflammation of the bladder and rectum. I hate hearing about all of this, sitting here trying to think objectively about the choices, trying to act as though I am not frightened. I squeeze Arlene's hand.

3) <u>Brachytherapy</u>. This is where they implant little radioactive seeds in your prostate gland. It has

the great advantage of minimal complications (With this disease, "complications" always mean the two I's, impotence and incontinence). Brachytherapy has the major disadvantage that the cure is not permanent. The cancer comes back in five or six years. That is far too soon to suit me.

4) <u>Radical prostatectomy</u>. This is "the operation." Bob Dole had it. Marion Barry had it. Timothy Leary, I suspect, did not have it and he is, right now, dying of prostate cancer on the Internet. Maybe LSD helps.

A radical prostatectomy takes a good surgeon an hour and a half or so to do. They slice down your midline from belly button to crotch, retract your bladder forward to expose the prostate gland, and cut it out in a block that includes the part of the urethra that traverses the gland. Then they implant the loose end of the urethra back into the bladder. You are in the hospital for three or four days, a catheter stays in your bladder for two weeks, no heavy exercise for six weeks, and then back to work. Piece of cake.

Not exactly. There are a couple of wrinkles in the scenario. First, everybody has some incontinence for a while. It goes away in ninety-eight percent of people. Those are pretty good odds. Impotence, inability to have a penile erection, is another matter.

The nerves that control the blood flow to the penis run right on top of the prostate gland. Those are the nerves critical to the function under discussion. If you cut those nerves, an unaided erection is impossible. If the cancer is very localized, you can do a "nerve-sparing procedure" where the surgeon carefully dissects the critical nerves off the gland before cutting it out. Even if you do that, thirty percent of people are still impotent after the surgery. And you don't know if you got all of the tumor until after the surgery, when the pathologist examines the tissue. The alternative is to remove the gland, nerves and all. One hundred percent impotence, but also a better chance for a complete cure.

I can imagine having prostate cancer. I cannot imagine being impotent. Apparently the operation leaves everything else—libido, sensations, even orgasm—intact. How totally weird.

God drives a hard bargain.

I have heard the term "neutral ground" used
only in New Orleans. Apparently the term originated
from when there were separate French and American
sections of the city. There was an island in the river
that was controlled by neither faction and where
neither's rules applied. The island is where people
met to do business. It was also the red light district.
Each transaction developed its own rules. It was
neutral ground. The term persists. For example, the
median in a boulevard is called neutral ground. I am
not sure, but I think the term is also used in a
symbolic, emotional sense. The sports metaphor
might be a level playing field.

   Although I was not born to it, I have been
enormously privileged. By hard work, reasonable
wit, and some luck, I attained a position in academic
medicine that commands considerable respect. I am
treated well, often perhaps better than I deserve, by
most people with whom I interact. None of that
matters right now. God is no respecter of persons.
Cancer meets me on neutral ground.

These two days blur together. Arlene and I talk a lot, mostly about the options. She loves me, and she has such good sense. We eat lunch somewhere downtown. We run five miles, across the river into East Nashville and back. There are long, uncharacteristic silences and uncharacteristically long faces. Arlene rarely overtly cries, but there are some tears now.

We discuss whom I should tell about this. Heather, of course, and the necessary people at work. Probably our artist friend, Myles Maillie. He is special to us, and if he had cancer I would want him to tell us; he would. I'm not sure about my sister, Elizabeth. I don't need to attract any more attention about this than is necessary. I have Arlene. This is our private problem, and we will solve it if it can be solved. If it cannot be solved, the last thing I need is a lot of attention.

Finally, we decide that having the maximum chance at a total cure is the most important thing to both of us—that time is more important than the technicalities of sexual intercourse—and that some of the potential treatments enabling penile erection might be acceptable. Arlene's argument is that if we went for the lesser operation with still a thirty percent likelihood of the same functional outcome and did not get all of the cancer, it would be devastating.

   While I obsess Wednesday afternoon on the thought of spending the remainder of my life impotent, Catherine calls. She wants to drop by. She has never done that. She has something to say.

   Catherine is a beautifully elegant, brilliant mother of four whom I have known for a long time. After divorcing her pathologist husband of many years, she married Michael. Michael had been a minister. He holds theological degrees and is a Greek and Hebrew scholar as well as a Biblical scholar. He is a daunting intellect, an accomplished public speaker, and a truly charismatic man.

   But it was discovered that Michael had a little problem which was not so compatible with his chosen profession. He has what has come to be called a "sexual addiction." It cost him his job, his marriage, and the respect of most of the people he knew.

   Catherine has a degree in Social Work, and she knew Michael through her church. She saved his life. She got him into counseling, they married and had what seemed to me a truly honest relationship. When they married, Michael was a construction worker. Not long after they married, he got into a financial business in sales. He rapidly ascended the corporate ladder, the company went public, and Michael became rich. They bought a million-dollar house and decorated it beautifully. They had elegant dinner parties with classical musicians.

Catherine drops by. She is really wired. She is divorcing Michael. It seems that the old problem was not cured after all—really not cured—and she discovered that only recently. It is very sad to be betrayed by one you love.

For the past few days, I have wrestled with the meaning of impotence to my relationship with Arlene. I am struck that potency can be an even bigger problem. What I really think is that neither is the most important thing in any love relationship worthy of the name. Arlene wonders later whether maybe Michael might benefit from a radical prostatectomy.

So many more important passions are evaded by sublimating them into sexual intercourse. Dennis Rodman and Madonna? Get real!

THURSDAY
MAY 16
Nashville

Back to work today. Call Jay Smith and get on
the op schedule for next Thursday if possible. Meet
with my chairman and break the news; present an
interim plan for directing the division. Tell some
people who need to know. Tell some other people
whom I want to know. Make a timetable for getting
everything necessary done before next Thursday.

I am exhausted. It feels as though I am
marching from one office to another discussing the
relationship between my prostate gland and God.
This no longer feels like neutral ground.

I need to make a list of all current issues facing
the division and their status. I am editing a book
that is already overdue, and several of the chapters
are not in; the publisher is hounding me. I have a
problem faculty member who needs a lot of
motivation and advice. A faculty candidate is
visiting from Bethesda, and I must host a dinner for
him. There are several issues to do with the budget
for the next fiscal year. There are faculty appointments, fellowship appointments, letters of

recommendation. There are data to review, experiments to plan, manuscripts to review, manuscripts to revise, grant applications to write, progress reports to get done. I need to cancel a talk that I agreed to give in Aspen in a couple of weeks. I am setting up a biotech company and that needs attention. The division is launching several new clinical initiatives requiring multiple levels of negotiations. There are probably a dozen other things that I can't remember right now.

And I have cancer, and the only reasonably sure cure will make me impotent.

There is an apocryphal story about an academician who was always on the road—giving talks, attending seminars. When asked who did his work at his home institution while he traveled, he replied: "The same people who do it when I am at home." I am surrounded by so many extraordinary people who care deeply for what we are about that everything that needs to be done in my absence will be done.

I tell my chairman that my greatest fear about being out for a while is that everyone will discover that they do not need me. He says, "Then you will have been the perfect administrator." "No," I say,

"the perfect administrator becomes totally super-
fluous without anyone realizing it."

Tonight I call Heather and tell her that I have
cancer. She is worried about renewing her driver's
license and figuring out how she can afford to leave
Daniel and live in New York. My cancer is
disappointed that it doesn't command more of her
attention. I am a little angry at her for not showing
that she cares. Arlene says that Heather probably
cares so much that she cannot deal with the feelings
head-on. I hope this is an opportunity.

FRIDAY
MAY 17
Nashville

Too much to do. Too little time.

MONDAY
MAY 27
MEMORIAL DAY
Nashville

It is Monday. It is Memorial Day. I have cancer, and I am scared. Tomorrow morning at 6:00 a.m. I am to check into Vanderbilt Hospital to have a radical prostatectomy at 7:30.

Heather was here over the weekend. It was good. I had some time to try to tell her what I am feeling. She is doing what she can to show how much she cares.

I spent last week at work telling people that I have cancer. It is exhausting work. Rehearsing repeatedly the history, the therapy, the prognosis, is physically exhausting. I guess it makes you deal with the specifics, expose every possible nuance of the process, but it is exhausting.

I can't finish the chapter today. It is my last chance to do it, but I can't.

David Baldwin has left a couple of messages in the past week. I determine to call him today, and I do. He had stomach cancer, and I talked with him a lot during that. Ironic. Now the tables are turned.

His voice is full of joyous caring Why should he care? I am very glad that he does.

I must tell Elizabeth. She is my sister. She is ten years older. She, too, watched prostate cancer consume our father. I call her and say the necessary words. She is sad. I say a lot of unnecessary words. Her voice breaks. My voice is strong and reassuring. Tears run down my cheeks. I mention Daddy and the pain. There are long silences. We hang up.

Arlene and I sit sipping very good bourbon on the porch in a rainstorm. We cry together. I am not afraid that Arlene will not love me cancer-free and impotent. I am afraid I won't be cancer-free, that the lymph nodes will be positive or that there will be no margins on the surgical specimens or that the damn PSA will not go to zero. Or that it will plummet only to rise, phoenix-like, from the devastation once again. Or that I will have trouble letting Arlene love me. I tell her all of that, and she holds me close.

I have diarrhea. It is the Dulcolax. Two Dulcolax tabs this morning and only clear liquids all day and nothing by mouth after midnight. The process is started. I am not hungry. I have cancer.

I have taken care of everything that I can. I am

not prepared to die, but neither am I sure that death requires much preparation. It is someone else's problem.

I do not expect to die. But I know that death is not always expected, even in the most controlled circumstances.

I am scared. If I did not have Arlene, I would not do this—I would just take my chances. It is odd that what makes me most want to live also makes me fear most the price of living. Thank the cosmic forces for Arlene's enduring sanity.

This is the final day in my life when I will be sexually potent. It all seems so technical. I do not believe in my head that either love or sex turns on technicalities. But the technicalities are not irrelevant.

In Arlene's arms I feel infinitely and unconditionally loved. But I am scared.

I just can't finish the chapter today. Don't worry. I will do it.

A handsome young medical student who came to my room at about five this morning to check my bowel sounds said it: "You are on the pathway." That is new jargon for medicine's current obsession with efficiency. Interesting to see it from this side. There is something comforting about knowing that there is a pathway and that I am on it.

I am surprised that the operation is easier than I feared. I thought the Foley catheter would be the worst thing, but I literally cannot feel the catheter. I have to look to know that it is there. The incision extending from my belly button to my crotch is sore, and there is a dull, full feeling in my pelvis. My brain didn't work quite right for about twenty-four hours, although I was not groggy, just couldn't focus very well. That was better yesterday afternoon. I was also out of bed and walking the halls with Arlene's help by yesterday afternoon. Sore, but not too bad.

Let me pause here to praise the morphine pump. They have an i.v. hooked up that you can control with a little button. When the button is pushed, it beeps and infuses a milligram of morphine. Contrary to popular conception, morphine is not an analgesic; that is, it does not relieve pain. But morphine causes you to view the pain differently, to see the pain as separate from yourself and not to care about it very much. *Beep-swoosh-aah.*

Fever last night. A chill just as Arlene was leaving, chilly all night, temp up to 100.8. Feeling cold and hot. I have been lying about blowing into the device they give you that is supposed to keep your lungs well-expanded; I have not been using it. With the fever I use it hourly all night, and the fever is down this morning. I would not have thought that a few little areas of collapsed lung would feel so much like an acute infection.

The psychological experience is more important than the physical one. Arlene and I talk about that. Jay says I no longer have cancer, and I believe that to be true. I have a lot of tubes in various natural and man-made orifices. I have a sore belly. But I probably do not have cancer. The hollow space in the middle of my chest seems to have filled. The tendency for my eyes to fill with tears when they meet Arlene's is gone. Although it makes my belly hurt, I can laugh again. The pain will go away. I trust the laughter will endure.

I called Heather yesterday at her work in New York. I wanted her to hear my voice, strong and clear. She was very happy to hear my voice. Neither of us is perfect, but we love each other.

Junior (Elizabeth's husband) called last night. Arlene talked with him. He rarely calls; it is always Elizabeth who calls. Despite the fact that we have no blood connection, Junior is my only real brother. I was moved that he called.

This morning I am not scared. Neutral ground.

JUNE 3
MONDAY
211 PRINTER'S ALLEY
HOME
Post-op day 6

Home on last Friday: right on the pathway. Less comforting to know that I'm on the pathway now, though, because I feel bad, have no energy, and hurt a lot. Jay said "moderate" blood loss. The truth is that my red blood cell count fell from 40 to 23. That means I lost three to four pints of blood, and I am severely anemic. Anemia makes me tired. I am not used to being tired. I do not like it. I take iron.

Pain does things to your head. Every time I move, I hurt. I am frustrated. I feel old. I look terrible in the mirror. I don't want Arlene to see me.

The excess fluid starts to mobilize on post-op day five. I lost three pounds in two hours. I lost five and a half pounds in twenty-four hours. It is wonderful to lose weight so quickly, but it is exhausting. I leaked around the catheter and wet my pants. I am fifty-six years old. I last wet my pants in grade school. I used to wet my bed as a child and was mortally embarrassed by that. I am, again, mortally embarrassed. I feel old. This was what I feared.

Tomorrow is Heather's birthday.

JUNE 5
WEDNESDAY
Home

Arlene has the distinct impression that middle-aged men have a proclivity for discussing their bowel habits to inappropriate excess. I swear to myself that I will never discuss my bowel habits with Arlene. I break the vow.

After any surgery in or around the abdomen, bowel habits assume extreme importance. While I was in the hospital, multiple layers of health care professionals inquired frequently and in salacious detail about bowel habits, carefully distinguishing between gas and the real thing. I felt like a two-year-old in potty training when I finally produced to a standing ovation from the team of white-coated voyeurs.

Thus rewarded, I find myself now broaching the

subject with Arlene. She is patient. She is not very interested. "This is important, an important part of my recovery," I say with more than a hint of indignity at her lack of interest.

"Yes, dear." She pats my hand.

The pain in my incision lasts longer than I would have thought. It still hurts to move. There are two distinctly different hurts. In the incision site there is an intense burning pain when I move. Then, deep in my pelvis, there is a dull, nauseating, visceral pain, mainly when I sit down.

I have established a morning and evening ritual with the catheter and associated paraphernalia. In the morning, I stay in bed and have coffee and read the paper until Arlene is finished in the bathroom and has gone to the front of the house. Then I get up, empty the large overnight collection bag, and attach a small, clean "leg bag" for the day. I then weigh myself, then rinse out the large bag and the leg bag removed the previous evening, and fill them with diluted vinegar. I leave the bags in the sink to soak until I finish showering. Then I empty the bags, rinse them thoroughly, and hang them in the shower to dry. Then I brush my teeth, shave, and dress. That completed, I am exhausted.

I am not as frightened of the catheter's demands since I made the ritual. Ritual has innate power. The process is separated from its substance so that going through the motions becomes the reason for going through the motions and thus is satisfying. There need be no importance to the process beyond the ritual. One does what one does. Neutral ground.

I called Heather yesterday to wish her happy birthday and to connect. She broke her foot, but it is getting better. She and Daniel, discovering that they cannot afford to live separately in New York (and I suspect discovering also that they don't really want to), are doing better, working on it. Heather asks how I'm doing, and I believe that she is really concerned. I tell her the truth. I'm tired and weak and sore, more so than I expected. But I am okay. We laugh a little about something. Arlene sits close beside me as I talk to Heather on the phone.

Some faxes from work. A grant I wanted to apply for is not possible because of a technicality. I don't care. Updates on several research projects, nothing earth-shattering. I start to worry again about work.

JUNE 6
THURSDAY
Home

It is probably noon. I just finished "the ritual." Arlene has gone to work for the afternoon. My incision still hurts, and now the catheter is starting to irritate my urethra so that I am conscious of the catheter most of the time; it is more annoying than painful. I need to call work to sort out a couple of minor things. I have done zilch on the chapter. Don't worry. I'll do the chapter.

Arlene is not religious. She is Ukrainian/Canadian, and her parents took her to the Russian Church in Winnipeg on special occasions when she was growing up. They also kept some rituals in their home. But Arlene does not believe in God.

That used to trouble me. I was brought up a strict fundamentalist Christian—church three times a week, no drinking, dancing, or "public bathing." I got over all of that somewhere along the way and am, even now, not totally clear with myself about my attitude toward potential Deity. I don't think that the God I was sold growing up is relevant to me anymore, so how much of that was "true" doesn't really matter much.

However, I have this fear that to dismiss totally the concept of a higher power is to take away any basis for a transcendent meaning to human life. I need to believe in the sanctity of human life. I asked Arlene once, early in our relationship, what she thought was the larger purpose of life, and with no pause she said, "To love and be loved." I know that to be true now.

But don't think it is easy. Arlene and I love each other, and each feels loved by the other. That happened because of who we are and how we went about relating to each other. Now I do not believe that there is another person on the planet whom I could possibly love as I do Arlene. I believe she feels the same way about me. I think that we had the extraordinary good fortune of encountering each other and that, had we not met, neither of us would ever have experienced a relationship like the one we have. But, even given that, to get to where we are took hard, painful, heart-wrenching, emotional work, countless hours of exploring ourselves and each other. A thorough and basic commitment to total honesty with each other is the only possible way that could be done. Honesty is hard.

It is comfortable now. I love and am loved, am able both to let myself be loved and to feel that. That does not emasculate cancer, does not prevent physical and emotional pain, does not alter the physiologic and psychological consequences of cutting out the nerves to the blood vessels in my penis, does not get chapters written or budgets balanced, does not raise my red blood cell count. But love puts those vagaries of everyday life in beautiful perspective. God is love, and SHe haunts the Neutral Ground.

The catheter goes next Monday. That will be nice. Also, the path report then. Surely Jay got it all. Surely!

JUNE 7
FRIDAY
Home

The recuperation at this point is more difficult
than the surgery. There is so much readjusting.
Absolutely everything about our lives is different
from before. I liked it the way it was. So did Arlene.

JUNE 8
SATURDAY
Home

    Arlene and I have two cats, Kelsey and Silko, given to us (and named) by Heather. Heather collects stray animals in New York.

    I do not believe that I am a "cat person" in the New Yorker sense of the term. I like cats all right. I can even appreciate their individuality. But before Kelsey and Silko I felt no strong empathy with cats.

    This past week I have spent a lot of time alone with our cats. I am somewhat frightened because I begin to understand cats. I do not mean by "understand" just observing and explaining behavior. I am beginning to resonate with the feline soul. Perhaps I am more receptive now without my prostate gland, cancer-free and impotent. Dark mysteries of the feline soul may be divined only by a peculiarly flawed few of us. I dare not write the mysteries down.

    It is raining. Arlene has gone to get litter for the cats. I feel stronger the last couple of days; no doubt the iron is kicking in. I had a bowel movement early this morning. I did not tell Arlene.

JUNE 9
SUNDAY
Home

We talked with Heather last evening, and she
and Daniel are going to join us at the Florida house
over the Fourth of July. We are excited about that.
Heather and Daniel have never visited the house in
Gainesville, and it will be good to share that
mesmerizing space with them.

Arlene built the house in Gainesville on sixteen
acres of prairie bordering wetlands while she was on
the faculty at the University of Florida. She had an
architect do it to suit her. The house is very
modern—clean, uncluttered lines—and sits in a
grove of ancient live oaks dripping Spanish moss.
You have to go a mile or so on a dirt road to get
there. Arlene used to call it her oasis. There is an
eagle nest out back and flocks of sandhill cranes
babbling constantly in the wetlands. We plan to
spend a couple of weeks there after I get the catheter
out and we get some loose ends dealt with here.
That should be a special time.

I thought I would be terminally bored during

this time, but I am not. My mind wanders about, skipping almost disinterestedly among topics. I just vegetate a lot. I concentrate on hurting sometimes, although I try not to do that too much. I think it important to feel the pain, but not to dwell on it. The pain will go away.

My mind drifts:

...still no progress on the chapter

...must see Jay tomorrow and get the catheter out (and the pathology report which I try very hard not to worry about today)

...on the pathway

Arlene went in to work this morning. She has an appointment for a pedicure at ten. Then she'll come home, and we'll go see Jay at one thirty, get the catheter out, and get the final path report.

I convinced Arlene to have her first pedicure several months ago, and now she is addicted. She has really great tootsies, and she keeps them appropriately beautiful. I think she does that for herself as well as for me.

It is hard to believe that I have not been to work for two weeks. The two weeks are hazy in my memory. When I read over what I wrote here, I can't remember much of it.

Elizabeth called yesterday, and I returned her call. She just wanted to know how I am doing. I told her the truth. I still hurt. The catheter is very annoying. I have too little energy. My brain is still not up to par. But I am all right. We chat a bit about Heather and Daniel and other family. I tell her I love her. I don't know if I have ever said the words to her before, although I am sure she knows it. The words open up a little floodgate of emotion from her. She says she loves me and that, although she doesn't call much, she hopes I know that she cares and that she is there for me if I need her. I say the same. We both know. The last time we had such an intimate conversation was when Arlene and I married—a joyous time. Blood connections thrive especially on pathos and joy.

Maybe once I get the path report and get rid of the catheter I can work on the chapter. Maybe not.

Jay pulled the catheter Monday afternoon, and it hurt like hell. The pain didn't last long. Now, two days later, I am virtually completely incontinent. I must wear those big diaper things all the time and change them frequently. Apparently the duration of the incontinence is unpredictable. It can last a few days to weeks to months. It is better than the catheter, but only just. It is hard to get much done when you are constantly concerned about whether you have wet your pants.

I think all this is starting to get to Arlene a little. I am encouraging her to go back to as full a schedule at work as possible. She is at work today. This is especially hard because, before I had cancer, we did absolutely everything together. Now she has to do most things alone while I mope about the house looking pained and constantly feeling my crotch.

Today begins the third week since Jay sliced open my belly and cut out the cancer while rearranging my pelvic anatomy. I am different than before that little episode. I don't know how much of it is just acute consequences of the surgery, the mechanics, and how much is having housed a nidus of immortality in my prostate gland and having had it unceremoniously whacked out. There surely are some cosmic implications of that process. God may not be pleased at such rude treatment.

Jay reviewed the path report with me on Monday. It appears as though there were clear margins, so the cancer should be all gone. The final test will be my PSA six weeks from now. It should be zero. If not, more options to discuss. I do not want to discuss any more options. Lately, there never is an option that I really like.

I felt terrible yesterday, mentally down. I'm a bit better today except when I first stand up and feel that warm, uncontrollable rush of urine seeping into my diaper. I constantly feel my crotch. I walk slowly and deliberately. I feel old. Arlene seems younger than ever to me.

I did read through Arlene's chapter for the book this morning. But I still haven't gotten back to mine.

We decided to postpone our trip to the Florida house by a week. We have a good bit to do to get ready for the trip, at home and at work. Also I would like to be a bit more active. It's a long drive.

JUNE 13
THURSDAY
Home

    Years ago, as a child, I had a recurring dream of being deeply submerged in water but being able to breathe normally. The dream was so real that when I went swimming, I believed that I really could breathe under water if I needed to. Fortunately, I never found it necessary to try.

    I am incontinent for the third consecutive day since the catheter was taken out. Water! What is the mystery of it? The incontinence affects my psyche out of proportion to the actual discomfort and inconvenience. The fact that I am incontinent is the center of my life. Dare I get up to get the book on the dresser across the room and risk the nauseating and uncomfortable sensation of urine rushing down my urethra? Do I have an incontinence pad with enough capacity to be able to walk a block to a restaurant for lunch with Arlene and not wet my pants? Water!

    I try to pretend that I am gaining some control by going rapidly to the toilet from a sitting position, thus availing my excretory system of the force of gravity. I change the pad frequently. I shower multiple times a day. But that subtle undercurrent of urine odor is always there. When I was fifteen and prostate cancer killed my father, he smelled like urine for a long time before he died.

I finished reading James Baldwin's *If Beale Street Could Talk*. Arlene and I visited Saint Paul d'Vence where J.B. lived and wrote. We talked of him (and Picasso, Yves Montand, Matisse, et al.) with Yvonne Roux, grande dame of the Colombe d'Or. She loved "Jimmy" and was particularly involved in the writing of *If Beale Street Could Talk*. She translated the book into French.

Baldwin writes so stunningly. I feel the unspeakable terror at being completely unable to influence events which are matters of life and death, the fear of doing everything right and, in spite of that, being wrongly victimized by the sheer arrogance of power. Cancer takes many forms. God need not be modest.

I am now reading *Tell Me How Long The Train's Been Gone*. It is dedicated to, among others, David Baldwin. I must call David.

Arlene talked on the phone for a long time with Heather last evening. I was very pleased.

Arlene went to work this morning and surprised me by coming home at noon. We walked a couple of blocks to Merchant's for lunch. We got a corner booth in the bar and had a lovely meal and conversation. Arlene is in good spirits today. I think I am getting more functional (except the incontinence), although the daily progress is frustratingly slow. I still haven't done much work-related stuff. (Don't ask about the chapter.)

I am reminded of John Irving's *Water Method Man*. I was amused when I read it some years ago. On reflection today I am less amused.

When Heather and Daniel married, they wrote their own vows. In the vows, Heather said she learned from me that "life does not have to be complex to be extraordinary." I thought that was very beautiful, but it surprised me. After digesting it some, though, I think that I believe that and somehow must have conveyed it to my daughter.

I think today that life need not be "complex" only given certain reliable assumptions. Or, more accurately, one need not be concerned with the complexities of life's infrastructure until they stop working. Cancer does that, messes up the works. Although I am doing almost nothing these days except going through the motions of existing, my life seems more complex than it has ever been. I can't assume anything—sufficient energy, control of my bladder, lack of pain—so I am reluctant to attempt very much.

But the complexities, even when you have to deal with them, are ordinary things. What makes life extraordinary is the ineffable beauty of simple things, like a sentence in your daughter's wedding vows that declares to you and the world a lesson learned without knowingly being taught.

Arlene tends her container garden on the deck. Her eyes brighten when she does that. A hot June day in Nashville. I am still incontinent, and it is five days since Jay pulled the catheter. I must call Heather today. She called the other night and left a message. She and Daniel may not be able to visit us at the Florida house. I am disappointed.

The people at GeneMedicine (a biotech company with whom we collaborate) sent me a get-well card signed by, I think, nearly everyone in the company. It is odd that one tends to be more moved by unexpected expressions of concern than by expected ones. Although I do not personally know the people at GeneMedicine very well at all, the unexpected card seemed more significant than the several expected ones from people whom I know much better. Caring, and saying so, are each important things to do.

I begin to feel tethered to this place.

I have never been afraid of flying. There is comfort in delegating responsibility appropriately. Having decided to board an airplane, one has decided to place one's fate in the hands of the pilot. It is the pilot's responsibility. If anything goes wrong, it is not my fault. I am very relaxed on an airplane, free of responsibility. I usually have no problem giving up control if responsibility goes with it.

On the surface, I would think flying an apt metaphor for surgery. You give up control. You place your life in someone else's hands. You are not responsible if something goes wrong. But I hope I never, never need to have surgery again. I find no comfort in giving up control and responsibility in that setting. The rules are different in matters involving a direct assault on your body. The whole process of preparing for, undergoing, and recuperating from surgery is permeated by an almost overwhelming sense of helplessness and humiliation.

I have spent my entire adult life in medicine, and you would think that good preparation for being a patient. It is terrible preparation. I hate the surly nurse's aid who takes my vital signs and am inclined to tell him so. I am annoyed by the parade of patronizing interns and residents who take a woefully inadequate history and listen to my chest perfunctorily through the hospital gown (the rasp of a hospital gown against the diaphragm of a stethoscope sounds like a typhoon, and you cannot hear heart and lung sounds in the middle of a typhoon). I hate the hospital gowns which always have the ties missing so that your ass is never covered (I usually spend a fair amount of time and effort assuring that my ass is covered). I both relish and abhor the pharmacology of Versed. Versed is an anesthetic that causes retrograde amnesia. They give it to you before surgery. You remember absolutely nothing from the time they wheel you to the operating room until you wake up in the recovery room. You do not remember the endotracheal tube, the anesthesia machine, the operating room banter...nothing. I love and hate Versed. Who knows what happened during those lost hours? My body was hideously violated in the presence of numerous accessories to the fact, and I have no ability to ruminate on that process, explore the cosmic implications. Versed took that away. And

Versed spared me the terror of remembered pain.

Three weeks today since surgery. A week and a day since the catheter was pulled. My energy level is markedly improved in the past couple of days. There is still some pain in the incision. I am fairly continent during the night, but when I am up and around I am totally incontinent still. This severely limits how far I will venture from the house— although I have recovered the pleasure of driving the Porsche, which lengthens the tether some. Arlene and I made a beautiful pasta last evening and ate by candlelight on the deck. There are many ways to make love.

I wet my pants. Damn!

JUNE 18
WEDNESDAY
Home

Angelo, my friend and colleague, gave me a book titled *The Artist's Way*. He meant to give it to me before the surgery, but there wasn't a chance. The book is basically a twelve-week course for discovering or rediscovering one's creativity. I read the introduction this morning. Generally, I think self-help books and creativity courses are bunk. But I am impressed with what I read in this one. I talked to Arlene about it. I am going to do the course. What can it hurt? I have always believed that the creativity that drives science is not different from that which drives art. The processes, too, are not that different. I am also receptive right now to using this time as an opportunity for renewal, a chance to sift through my life and opportunities, to select and burnish the creative nuggets and get rid of the garbage.

I worked some on the chapter yesterday. I plan to go in to work for half a day tomorrow if my incontinence permits. It may well not. We still plan to go to the Florida house next week. I feel stronger every day. I love Arlene. There are many ways to express that. I believe that she is happy. Bo Sheller is coming over this afternoon allegedly to discuss some experiments that he is planning. My guess is that he just wants to come by to make me feel involved in the work. Bo has been and is a dear, dear friend.

JUNE 20
FRIDAY
Home

I went to work for half a day yesterday. While straining some with a bowel movement, I suddenly felt a ripping in my pelvis inside the suture line. I thought the surgical incision had ripped open. There was an intense burning pain. I was terrified. I looked at the wound and felt it, and I could not identify a defect. The suture line in the skin appeared to be intact. I still don't know what happened, but something did. My abdomen is sorer today, although I think the incontinence is some better.

Bo did come by Wednesday afternoon. It was late in the day, and Arlene had not come home from work. I had been alone all afternoon and was feeling more than a little sorry for myself. I did not feel like entertaining company. Bo came. I made us martinis. He brought me a book (very light reading, although Bo was a Rhodes Scholar and an English major at Sewanee). We sat and just talked generally for a bit. I caught him up on my illness and plans. We discussed the mouse experiments he was planning.

Bo is smarter than I am, but, fortunately, I don't think he knows that. I intend to do all I can to perpetuate his illusion. He did not need my advice about the experiments, but I am certain that seeking my advice was not a ruse for trying to distract me from my illness. He really wanted my advice. I gave it to him. My advice was that he do exactly what he had planned to do before consulting me. He thought that was brilliant advice. So do I. I very much enjoyed the visit with Bo, and I am glad he came by.

I once told Arlene that she gives easier than she takes. I think that is true, but taking is the hardest part of any relationship, including friendship. During my illness so many people have expressed genuine concern. The hardest part is accepting and relishing the love and concern of other people, and, paradoxically, letting yourself be loved is the most you can give to another person. I am reminded by Bo's visit how good a friend he is. Bo gives so lavishly and with such perception. He has a lot of trouble taking. Maybe he'll grow into it. I hope it doesn't take a cancer. Some more ordered growth would be much preferable.

I have decided to do the creativity course starting Sunday.

I decide that a fifty-six-year-old, post-radically-prostatectomized, incontinent, impotent, and presumably cancer-free man need be in no great hurry to coddle his inner artist child. Having thus decided, I did not start *The Artist's Way* course on Sunday. I put it off. My inner artist child can cool his or her heels in the anteroom a bit longer.

I went to the Y with Arlene today for the first time since surgery (now into the fifth post-operative week) and walked two and a half miles on the treadmill. It felt pretty good. The worst discomfort was that incontinence pads are hot and the mixture of sweat and urine trapped next to stubby, regrowing pubic hair becomes terribly itchy. It felt nice to get a little exercise again.

The movers came today and loaded the stuff we are taking to the Florida house. We plan to go there on Friday. It will be exciting to get the place adequately furnished and to get some of our art there. I suspect we will go there more often now. I got my laptop rigged for the Internet, so I can stay in touch with everyone via E-mail from wherever there is a phone. I played with it some. It will let me actually accomplish some work while we are in Florida. Electronics can take away any connection between place and function. I wonder what that does to the psyche of a Southerner, imbued from birth with the inviolable sanctity of one's sense of place. Cyberspace is so glaringly intangible, an ultimate abstraction. The scary part is that it works.

Arlene and I had dinner at Sole Mio last evening. Wonderful nitti and penne and a delightful basil-drenched carpaccio appetizer. We saw Manuel and Janice Zeitlin there. Manuel is an architect who is designing a renovation of our Printer's Alley home. He and Janice are really neat people with whom both Arlene and I resonate.

I wet my pants again...damn!

The afternoon sun casts latticed shadows through our porch rail. White cascading petunias, pink begonias, ochre-festooned giant gold daisies in a pot, contorting midget evergreens, six kinds of herbs—Arlene's carefully selected and pampered flora—devour the sun and smile. My Valentine wind chime tinkles now and then. Arlene, hair still wet from the shower, sits reading Dickens. I have done almost no work-related things in four and a half weeks. The sun and love are warm. In the distance I fancy that I hear the faint whimper of my inner artist child.

TUESDAY
JULY 9
The Florida house

Six weeks ago this morning I lay blithely in the amnesic arms of Versed as Jay Smith mucked about in the innards of my pelvis. I bear still the physiologic consequences of his work and, I pray, the anatomic consequences as well.

I awake this morning to the soft hiss of a steady rain. Birds which I do not recognize sing recognizable songs. Beyond the open doors, vivid greens, many shades, glow in the morning light. I nestle next to Arlene among the sweeping ancient arms of live oaks around the bedroom windows.

This is good time. Healing time. There is a spiritual part to healing. I doubt that the pathway considers that. This place, serene but for the gentle grinding of Nature's wheels, is haunted by the spirits of countless living things, spirits unfettered by the careful dimensions with which I usually confine my life.

We are here now almost two weeks. I have done no work on the chapter. I have communicated some by phone and E-mail and FedEx with the office, but not much really. John Oates called the other day from Nashville just to connect, without an agenda. I am not used to dealing much with John without an agenda. It was a very good conversation.

I did not start *The Artist's Way* course yet. I think about it. I reflect on the parts of the book that I have read. I may get to the structured part, and I may not. I don't often do very well with imposed structure. I have my own structure that is commonly not very apparent, but that usually works for me. I may do the course, though.

I had a long telephone conversation with Heather last night, late. For the first time during my illness, she verbalized her concern and asked all of the questions that I wanted her to ask much earlier. She also asked if I am mad at her. There is a lot of non-verbal connection between us which can obscure the issues. We love each other, though. Love covers a multitude of sins.

The decision to spend this time here is a very good one. It is healing time for Arlene, too. She loves this land. She must have been a farmer in another life.

Medical crises spread such broad emotional tentacles. I think this is easier for me than for Arlene, despite her incurable sanity and good judgment. I have something quite tangible to deal with. But for Arlene the pain is more diffuse and the pathway undefined. She has to blaze a trail and can depend less on me for help than either of us would like.

We are healing. We will return to Nashville on Friday and plan to start work full-time the following Monday. I am changed, without my cancer, impotent and incontinent. I trust the changes will integrate amiably.

Although impotent in the technical sense, I had a lovely orgasm the other day.* Well-motivated and creative people can devise imaginative solutions to many difficult problems.

*Having an orgasm does not require an erection.

WEDNESDAY
JULY 9
The Florida House

I wet my pants again without realizing it last evening. We sat in the living room. I was half into my second martini. It hadn't happened for a while. I was depressed again. The experience triggers an emotional response much larger than the facts deserve. The feelings are helplessness, embarrassment, like a small child. And the latent fear that I am, in fact, still ill. That the cancer is still there somewhere and that the ever-present smell of urine is, as I recall it, the harbinger of a dark fate. Maybe the whole business of medicine is a futile effort to thwart the inevitable. We are, after all, mortal. If I am cured of prostate cancer, I will die of something else. I hope it smells different.

THURSDAY
JULY 10
The Florida house

Celinda Pink sings her earthy elegance to me from the Bang and Olufsen stereo. We like Celinda Pink. We love her flawed passion.

I reflect, to Celinda's rhythms, on *The Artist's Way*. I reflect because my friend Angelo gave the book to me. It is written by a screenwriter who teaches courses for various kinds of artists who feel the need to rejuvenate their creativity. The author figures she knows how to put such people back on track. I suppose she does. She makes a living at it.

From the bit I have read so far, it seems that the major premise is that within each creative person there is an inner artist child. Many external pressures (and some inner, left-sided ones) tend to exclude the inner artist child from most of the action. The secret to remaining creative is to resist those pressures, to let the artist child, the "Little Prince," live and work through your otherwise thoroughly functional and respectable self.

Okay. But do I need the course spelled out so precisely over twelve weeks? I'm not sure. I wonder whether I give over my life so completely to my inner artist child that I neglect the rest of me. Maybe my inner artist child is a spoiled brat who has been too much indulged and could benefit considerably from a good whack on the derriere. I don't see where *The Artist's Way* ponders that possibility. I don't like courses anymore. I have done so many courses.

This place, this land, is not neutral ground. This is ground hallowed by Arlene's love and sweat. She sought it, found it, loved it, and presented it to me to love with her. This is our ground. True, God had a hand in making it, and Bertha or Caleb or Deborah could veer across the peninsula and alter this ground dramatically. But not so dramatically as to spoil the beauty. Beauty is more powerful than pain.

The babble of a sandhill crane moves my mind elsewhere.

We head north tomorrow, toward reality. I am changed. I am interested to see how that translates into my life. I am anxious to know how long I will be incontinent. I am anxious to discover what clever devices the urologists have made to deal with what I am certain they perceive as a purely mechanical problem. I am very anxious to know that my PSA has gone to zip.

We go to Amelia's, in town, to dinner tonight. There are special memories. We dress up for the occasion. We celebrate life and love tonight. I am not sure how many extra pads to take with me. I desperately hope that I do not soil my Armani pants. The smell. I need to repress the haunting smell.

FRIDAY
JULY 11
The Florida house

Before dinner at Amelia's last evening, we stop for a drink at The Sovereign. Sometime in the past, we went there after dinner. There was jazz and erudite conversation in the lovely bar, down a long brick corridor with carriage lamps. Tonight there is a private party. Someone's fiftieth wedding anniversary. A lot of old people. The bartender is nervous and has us sit to the side with the regulars. The regulars are four lawyers drinking martinis and talking shop. Too many words said too loudly. I say to Arlene that we will not live to celebrate fifty years together. I dislike that thought, but it is true.

We sit at the same table by the window at Amelia's where we sat for two hours over lunch on a Saturday when Arlene had to take me to the airport for a flight back to Nashville. We remember those times. We are happy to be together for good.

I walk through the house admiring our handiwork. We have made this place our home now, too. The art is hung. The stereo is in place, beautifully comfortable under the living room window. The kitchen is equipped and used. I made bread. I made pasta. We chopped leeks together. The place is beautiful.

I did not appreciate before being here how much Arlene loves physical work. She cannot stop busying herself with a thousand chores. I always thought her more of an intellectual than I. Maybe not. Or maybe I'm just lazier.

The only two places in the world where I have consistently found Bunnahabain whiskey are Scotland and Gainesville, Florida.

MONDAY
JULY 22
Nashville

Today begins the second week that I am back at work full-time. Today is also six weeks since my catheter was pulled. I remain incontinent when I am active, although at night or when sitting I am fairly dry. I also remain disappointed and intermittently frustrated by the incontinence.

The odd thing about returning to work is that it does not feel like I was away for seven weeks. Things have happened, but things happen when I'm here. It doesn't seem to matter very much. That is good. I won't be here forever, and there are too many good people and too good a program for too much to depend on my being here.

I am back into serious exercise this past week, and that helps—one more piece of normalcy fit back into our disrupted lives. The familiar puzzle is gradually, piece by piece, being reassembled. But the emerging picture is not quite the same. It is as though someone repainted the surfaces of the same jigsaw pieces. We will not know what the picture is until the last piece finds its niche.

A big piece or two comes this week. I see Jay Smith at ten this morning. He is to discuss with Arlene and me the urologists' options for dealing with impotence (right now the incontinence is a greater deterrent to sex than impotence). I can hardly wait.

I presume that I will also have blood drawn for a PSA today. That means I should know this afternoon or tomorrow whether I still have cancer. I am anxious to know that. I am still frightened. It is hard to believe that the Fates can be thwarted by so soul-less and mechanical an exercise as surgery. Perhaps it is the pain that frightens Fates away.

I made bagels yesterday for the first time. They didn't sink in the water when I boiled them, so I must have let them rise too much the second time. But they were very good. Arlene and I ate them with fresh Romano for dinner while watching the Olympic gymnastics on television. It was a good time.

I do not have cancer.

Jay told me that last Monday, reviewed the final path report with me. There was one little glitch, some capsular invasion at one site, but Jay says that is almost always artifact. The PSA came back Tuesday undetectable. I do not have cancer.

A weight is lifted from our lives. The right things were done. The outcome was right. I recognize that the one does not always assure the other, but there is confidence in seeing events follow the laws of cause and effect, especially in biology where things don't always make such obvious sense.

I no longer have cancer, but I am not the same person I was before I had cancer. There are the persisting consequences of the surgery. But there is more. The entire experience of negotiating with Fate when the deck seems to be stacked and coming out on top does something in addition to the surgery.

The path report says the main tumor was two by one by one centimeters. Jay calls that a moderate size. I begin to have some serious doubts about Jay's quantitative abilities. I bled down three pints at surgery, and he calls that "moderate" blood loss. The tumor is as big as half a normal prostate gland, and he calls that a "moderate" size. I call it big. We are both amazed that it took so many biopsies to find it. But that little piece of immortality is sitting pickled in a jar in the surgical path lab, and my zero PSA says that my body contains no prostate tissue of any sort, mortal or immortal.

I do not have cancer. The incontinence is improving some, right on the pathway. The smell is still with me, an invisible vaporous cloud permeating my world. But the cloud is not so ominous now. It will go away, and I will not die of prostate cancer.

My father's cancer was diagnosed when he was about sixty-two. I presume it was metastatic when discovered. I was only about twelve, but as I recall he had transurethral surgery and brachytherapy. I almost certainly had exactly the same disease, but then there was no blood test. My prostate was totally normal to physical examination. Without the PSA, my cancer would probably have been dis-covered, metastatic, in my sixties. Like my father, I would have died at sixty-five, a horrible wasting dehumanizing death, angry at God and all humankind and, always, reeking of urine. The advances achieved by medical research over the past forty years spared me that fate. I am proud to be a part of that exhilarating and noble process of discovery. It is money, time, and energy well-spent.

There is this little problem of impotence. There are some other options, but Jay suggests to start with "Farmer Osbon's Wonderful Erection Machine."

Jay tells us this story for the truth. It seems that several years ago there was a farmer in Georgia who was impotent. Farmers, at least successful ones, are problem solvers and entrepreneurs, and they are not at all daunted by the mechanics of sex. Breeding farm animals involves an entire armamentarium of procedures, devices, and manipulations of the animal psyche to assure the fruitful marriage of sperm and egg.

So Farmer Osbon figures that if the penis won't fill up from the inside, maybe you could inflate it from the outside. He made a big tube with a vacuum pump on one end that could fit over the penis, pump it up with a vacuum, and then keep it up by putting a rubber band around the base of the penis to hold the blood in until you were ready to let it down. He made the device and used it, and it worked.

Farmer Osbon had two young daughters. He packed up his machine and two daughters and went to a national urologists meeting, set up a booth, and hawked his wares. He wore his farmer overalls. Apparently he and his device were the big urologist joke of the meeting.

Farmer Osbon is dead now, but his heirs are, undoubtedly, all multimillionaires. The current generation of his device is one of the most popular and successful means of dealing with impotence in the world.

Arlene and I agree that we will try Farmer Osbon's machine. In its modern packaging, complete with video instructions, it cost in 1996 about three hundred dollars.

SUNDAY
AUGUST 11
PRINTER'S ALLEY
Nashville

Sex is one of those things that is better done than talked about. Sex is quintessential nonverbal communication. When one tries to put words to the music, dissonance is inevitable. Arlene and I talk sometimes about sex, but mostly without words.

I find myself now compelled to talk about sex with people whom I hardly know. I have enormous respect for Jay Smith as a urologist, but I hardly know him, and I am acutely uncomfortable discussing my sex life with him. The same goes for his nurse.

Also, the discussions seem all wrong. The discussions are all about mechanics, which never before seemed an issue to me. If the magic is there the mechanics take care of themselves.

But not when you whack out those blessed vasomotor nerves. The magic does not require the nerves, but the amount of blood retained in the erectile tissue of the penis is controlled by nerves. And nerves are necessary to translate the magic into its natural mechanical consequences. Nerves whacked, it becomes necessary to effect that translation by extraordinary contrivance. The extraordinary contrivance in widest use is Farmer Osbon's Wonderful Erection Machine.

The machine is awkward and ugly, but it works. That is, it works in the technical sense— produces, over the course of a few minutes, a reasonably erect penis which will stay that way for a bit when the rubber band is placed around its base.

As a transducer of sexual magic, however, Farmer Osbon's Wonderful Erection Machine leaves something to be desired.

MID-SEPTEMBER
1996
Nashville

There is a group of chemicals called prosta-
glandins, originally discovered in the prostate gland
(thus their name), but made by most cells in the
body. It was recently discovered that over about
fifteen minutes after injecting prostaglandin E (PGE)
into the side of the penis, the penis becomes quite
erect and stays that way for around an hour and a
half.

I first learned of this effect upon reading an
article on the pornographic movie industry in the
New Yorker magazine. A penile erection on the part
of the male lead is a necessary prerequisite to
beginning filming, and such does not always happen
on cue. This can delay filming and increase
production costs; it is an economic problem. In the
industry it is called "waiting for wood." When the
wait gets inordinately long, injection of a cc of PGE
into the side of the penis allows the show to get on
the road.

Now, PGE is approved as a treatment for
impotence. It comes packaged in little blue plastic

individual dose packs with a syringe, alcohol swabs, everything you need. Inserting the small needle into the side of the penis is essentially painless, and it works as advertised. The only minor problem is waiting for wood to go away. However, it is not too difficult to keep occupied during that period.

Another piece of the puzzle slips into its niche. It fits, although the picture is a little different.

LATE SEPTEMBER
1996
The Florida house

Yesterday was Arlene's birthday, and she wanted
to spend it here, together and away from inter-
ruptions in our togetherness. We are together as we
never were.

I choose to remember this season past as "The
Summer of the Crab."* I have always been in touch
with my flaws, but I thought them mostly meta-
physical. A cheek-to-jowl encounter with physical
vulnerability is another matter, a matter not readily
ignored even for the briefest time. My body reminds
me, still, of the encounter. The literal scar bisecting
my lower abdomen and the functional consequences
of what went on beneath it are not the stuff of
poetry, not grist for the metaphysics mill.

But now—painless, cancer-free, and forever
changed—I do see some magic in "The Summer of
the Crab." The magic shows itself in fits and starts.

*crab is doctor jargon for cancer, after the astrological sign

There is no need to continue this journal. The angst that fathered it is dead: a nodule of tissue half the size of an English walnut sitting, pickled now, in a jar on a shelf in the Department of Surgical Pathology at Vanderbilt University Hospital.

To close this story I will contemplate some things I learned (or relearned) during the past few months.

LESSONS
from the
SUMMER
OF THE CRAB

- This entire planet is Neutral Ground for Homo sapiens—wars, megamergers, toys, money, and sexual conquests to the contrary notwithstanding. We all are in the business of life together, and the Fates do not play favorites in any way that you can count on.

- Cancer, even at its most hideous, is only an annoying aside. Tragedy is to grow old unloved and unloving. We will all die. Life is a fatal proposition. Love is more than life and does not recognize mortality.

- If you must ever choose between incontinence and impotence, choose impotence. Impotence is a periodic inconvenience for which there are remedies. Incontinence occupies your mind at every moment, and you cannot escape the smell.

- Do not contract a potentially fatal disease that killed your father. If you do, deal with the whole thing promptly.

- The human organism is, both emotionally and physically, extraordinarily resilient. The grossest insults heal so that functions persist. But there are scars; healing is not a perfect process.

- Sex is complex in ways beyond the ability of humans to analyze in any meaningful way. Carpe diem.

- No conspiracy of the Fates can rob you of the beauty you can see. No equal power can show you the beauty beyond your vision.

- When you become ill (it is inevitable), God grant you a good doctor. Like a good woman, his price is above rubies.

- While it is not possible to make life simple, it is possible to relish life's simplicities.

- Learn to be gentle with yourself and the Fates will acquiesce.

- Rarely, in matters of consequence, can you call the tune, but you can always choose your partner. That is more important.

- If you live in a house of cards, the quicker you discover that the better. Pay attention.

- If you are unsure of what you feel, learn from what you do. The two are linked inextricably.

- Immortality is probably not all it is cracked up to be. Life force out of control is hell-bent for catastrophe.

- Aging is a concept. The concept is based on an inexorable course of things, but it needn't encumber your brain.

- Happiness is an attitude, as is misery. It's really up to you.

- I understand, now, the human race's endless fascination with experimental pharmacology.

- As a person, strive to be ordinary. Most extraordinary things are done by ordinary people. To be unique is to be alone.

- It is probably not critical to stay between the lines, but it is probably critical to know where your lines are.

- Be still and listen.

- Pain, at its worst, is less important than the expectation and the memory. The same may be true of pleasure at its best.

- There are few words wiser than the babble of a sandhill crane.

- Anticipate ecstasy, not disaster, if you must anticipate at all. Even if disaster happens, you have had the pleasure of the foreplay.

JULY 22, 2000
SATURDAY
Printers Alley

I entered the new millennium with a PSA of zero, four years out from the surgery. I do not have and will never have prostate cancer. I will die of something else.

Good and bad things happen, the one no less real than the other. It is not possible to excise the bad from life, like cutting out a cancer; good and bad are opposite sides of the same coin.

On a sunny afternoon someone killed Skull Schulman, slit his throat and left him to die alone in a pool of his own blood on the floor of the Printers Alley bar that bore his name. I do not understand gratuitous violence.

Prostate cancer killed Timothy Leary.

My friend Angelo betrayed me for no good reason. I trusted him. I do not understand betrayal.

Junior died. Elizabeth dealt with his death with dignity and strength that I did not know she had.

Heather and Daniel divorced. Heather now lives in Providence, works at Brown, and is finishing up school. Her friend, Josh, seems a good person with whom she shares a lot. She is happier than I can recall her being. She needs me less than ever, and I think we are better friends than we have ever been. I am proud of Heather.

Arlene turns fifty this year, and we are going to spend a month in Venice to celebrate. We have taken a flat and invited people we care for to visit us there. Our new and special friends, Mark and Anne Manner, are coming, and our old and dear friend Richard Parker; and Heather and Josh, Myles Maillie, and Richard and Lorna, Arlene's brother and his wife. Manuel and Janice Zeitlin can't come, but maybe next time. I hope Elizabeth can come, but I understand if she cannot. It will be very good time.

The blue diamond cured my impotence; that little pill rescued Bob Dole and me from having to choose between celibacy and contrivance. The little blue diamond not only takes care of the technicality but also restores the magic. Bob and I are fortunate to be alive at all, but especially fortunate to be alive now.

Doug Milam, Jay Smith's colleague, is taking care of my incontinence by injecting collagen at critical sites. It is working. I imagine the inside of my bladder neck looking like Julia Roberts' lips.

On a lovely Saturday afternoon, Arlene and I drive to Franklin just to be together and enjoy the day. We eat lunch at a quaint old restaurant on Main Street. We order a bottle of champagne, and when the young waiter brings it he says, "This must be a special day."

"Yes," I reply. "Every day is a special day."

ABOUT THE AUTHOR

Kenneth Larry Brigham, M.D., is Ralph and Lulu Owen Professor of Pulmonary Medicine, Director of the Center for Lung Research, and Chief of the Division of Allergy, Pulmonary, and Critical Care Medicine at Vanderbilt University School of Medicine. He has authored more than two hundred articles in professional journals and has edited three scientific books. He is a former president of the American Thoracic Society and currently serves on the editorial board of the American Journal of Respiratory Cell and Molecular Biology and as Executive Editor of Respiratory Research. In recent years Dr. Brigham's research has focused on gene therapy for lung diseases. In addition to his University role, he serves as President of geneRx+, a biotechnology company that he founded in 1998 in an effort to translate laboratory discoveries more rapidly into practical treatments for human disease.

Dr. Brigham was born the last of three children to Alvin Dixon and Josie May Everett Brigham in the front bedroom of a four-room house at 1120 North Seventh Street in a modest East Nashville neighborhood on October 29, 1939. He grew up in rural Middle Tennessee, attended public school, and received a B.A. degree from David Lipscomb College and an M.D. degree from Vanderbilt. He subsequently received further professional training at Johns Hopkins Medical School and the University of California San Francisco and served two years in the U.S. Public Health Service. He returned to the Vanderbilt faculty in 1973 and has spent his entire professional career there.

Hard Bargain is Dr. Brigham's first book published for a general audience.